General Fund 10.95
1989-90

WEST LEYDEN ELEMENTARY LIBRARY

UNDERWATER SPECIALISTS

BY
Shirley Keran

EDITED BY
Anita Larsen

PUBLISHED BY
CRESTWOOD HOUSE
Mankato, MN, U.S.A.

CIP

LIBRARY OF CONGRESS CATALOGING IN PUBLICATION DATA

Keran, Shirley.
  Underwater specialists.

  (At risk)
  Includes index.
  SUMMARY: Examines the history, techniques, equipment, and dangers of underwater occupations, including salvage divers, lockmen divers, and diving scientists.
    1. Diving, Submarine—Juvenile literature. [1. Diving, Submarine. 2. Occupations.] I. Larsen, Anita. II. Title. III. Series.
  VM984.K47   1988   627'72—dc19   88-14890

  ISBN 0-89686-400-6

International Standard Book Number:	Library of Congress Catalog Card Number:
0-89686-400-6	88-14890

PHOTO CREDITS

Cover: Tom Stack & Associates: Ed Robinson
Wide World Photos, Inc.: 13, 14, 20, 22-23, 43
Third Coast Stock Source: (MacDonald Photography) 8, 17; (Jim Kissinger) 10
DRK Photo: (Doug Perrine) 7, 18, 36-37; (Robert Holland) 33, 34
Tom Stack & Associates: (Ed Robinson) 4, 28-29, 31, 38, 39; (M. Timothy O'Keefe) 25

Copyright © 1988 by Crestwood House, Inc. All rights reserved. No part of this book may be reproduced in any form without written permission from the publisher, except for brief passages included in a review. Printed in the United States of America.

Produced by Carnival Enterprises.

Box 3427, Mankato, MN, U.S.A. 56002

TABLE OF CONTENTS

Underwater Adventures....................................5
Today's Divers..6
Breath-Holding Divers....................................9
Ancient Diving Devices..................................10
Diving Bells, Buckets, and Barrels.....................11
Underwater "Hard Hats"................................13
Diving "Boxes"..14
The Bends..15
Deep Diving Narcosis....................................16
Modern SCUBA...18
Tows and Tenders..19
Wet Subs...19
The Buddy System..21
"Lockmen" Divers...26
Off-Shore Oil Divers......................................27
Salvage Divers...31
Diving Scientists..32
Marine Animals That Sting or Bite.....................38
Diving Takes Training....................................40
Sport Diving..41
Looking Ahead Down Below............................42
For More Information....................................45
Glossary/Index..46-48

UNDERWATER ADVENTURES

The diver came up from the water and lifted his diving mask. Everything had changed! The sky was a sickly yellow. The water of the Gunflint River was dead calm and as grey as its name. "Let's head out!" he shouted, hoisting himself into the boat.

But before underwater archaeologist Robert Wheeler and his partner could reach safety, the storm hit. Gusting winds overturned their small boat. The two men clung to the hull. Again and again, winds slammed them against their boat's side with such force that Wheeler broke seven ribs.

Wheeler took risks like this to recover objects like an iron musket, a copper kettle, or a string of beads from underwater sites.

"Would you do it again?" he was asked.

Wheeler's answer was, "Yes, it was all worth it." He said objects found along inland waterways explain this country's history. The objects tell of a time when Native American traders and French Canadian voyageurs paddled lakes and rivers in canoes. Simple clay pipes or fancy silver armbands record the trade that opened up the North American continent.

The underwater world lures people from all walks of life. They may dive for knowledge, profit, or

Curiosity about the fascinating underwater world draws many people to diving.

adventure. Curiosity—the thirst to know—is a powerful motive for going underwater. But diving is also a challenge. Underwater, things are not always what they seem.

Craig Roberts, a SCUBA diver and surfer, knows this. His fiberglass surfboard is missing a chunk. Craig thinks the 17-foot white shark that gobbled that fiberglass looked up and mistook man and board for a seal. Craig says, "Once you enter the water, you enter the food chain."

Today, scientists, mechanics, engineers, doctors, photographers, and sport enthusiasts dive. It's a good thing they do. Without the diver, we would know far less about many forms of sea life. We would have no human sightings of underwater volcanoes and mountains that one day may help explain the origins of Earth.

With good training, equipment, and practice, anyone can dive and explore the fascinating world that lies underwater.

TODAY'S DIVERS

Today's divers go underwater for as many reasons as others work on land or in air. Professional divers specialize. They may be medics, mechanics, photographers, carpenters, welders, or electricians.

Some are scientists. They may be archaeologists

Once in the water, divers must realize that they become part of the food chain!

studying ancient shipwrecks, biologists studying marine life, or geologists helping to find oil. Geographers go underwater to map the sea bottom. Oceanographers study underwater volcanoes.

Divers can be civilians who dive to earn money, or they can be members of the armed forces. Others are teachers, training others to dive. Many men, women, and children dive for the fun of it.

One version of the ancient "sink stone" is a heavy diving helmet.

BREATH-HOLDING DIVERS

Scientists have found that men dove as far back as 600 B.C. The Greek poet Homer tells about a charioteer who fell off his horse. According to Homer, a spectator said: "How well he dives! If we had been at sea, this fellow would have dived from the ship's side and brought up as many oysters as the whole crew could stomach."

How would a person in 600 B.C. dive? By holding his breath! Breath-holding still continues today in parts of the world. Pearl divers in the Indian Ocean hold their breath as they gather oysters from the ocean bottom. Some of these divers hold out a flat, heavy stone to "aim" their underwater descent. Others dive with a 40-pound stone attached to a cord that is tied around their bodies. This "sinkstone" weighs down the diver and keeps him close to the sea bottom.

Pearl divers can hold their breath for 80 seconds and longer while they work. They scoop pearl oysters into a basket hung from a rope. A partner on top watches the cord. When it's time for the divers to come up, the sinkstone is hauled up first. Next the basket of pearl oysters is hoisted up. Finally the diver can come up for air.

In shark-infested waters of the Indian Ocean, divers wear sinkstones and carry an ironwood spike for protection. Before they go down, however, a shark charmer riding in the boat chants prayers for the safety of the divers!

ANCIENT DIVING DEVICES

Long ago, divers tried different devices to help them breathe underwater. One device was a "breathing bag" made of sheep or goat skin. It hung beneath a diver's stomach with a tube that reached his mouth. The breathing bag might help a diver get air, but it wouldn't help him stay submerged!

Snorkeling is a starting point for all beginning divers!

Another device was a reed, or breathing tube, about 12 inches long. The top of the reed was kept above water. The diver could swim under the water's surface as long as he breathed through the bottom of the reed. Divers often used reeds to hide just below the surface of the water and sneak up on enemy ships.

DIVING BELLS, BUCKETS, AND BARRELS

Throughout history, divers have been used in fighting wars. Back in 332 B.C., Alexander the Great had a whole army of divers. In one battle, Alexander had his soldier-divers gather rocks and stones from a fallen city to build a massive breakwater. The breakwater became a bridge to his new conquest — an island.

Divers have also harvested oysters, coral, kelp, sponge, or searched for sunken treasures. Whatever the task, divers needed strength and endurance. Even so, they often didn't live long because of poor diving equipment.

A diving apparatus was needed. Merchants wanted to recover sunken ships and cargoes. Port cities wanted to build harbors and bridges. Kings wanted to fortify waterways. All of these things required divers to spend longer and longer periods of time underwater.

Someone had an idea: Why not suspend a strong tub from a strong rope into the water? A large, sturdy tub was found, and weights were attached to sink it upside down. Because air was trapped inside, the diver was able to stay underwater for several hours. He could even leave the tub for short periods to work—if he held his breath. The tub was called a "diving bell." The name is still used today, but the device has changed a lot.

Sir Edmund Halley made some of the first changes. He put weighted barrels of air inside to re-supply the bell's atmosphere. Halley was able to spend over four hours at a depth of 66 feet.

About the same time, in 1715, John Lethbridge made a leather-enclosed diving "case" that could be used by one person. Like the diving bell, the case was slung from a ship. A diver could work to a depth of 60 feet for about 30 minutes.

Diving bells with or without barrels and buckets were not perfect. Divers could not move about freely. They needed a steady air supply. A pump that could deliver air under pressure was needed. The pump would force air down to the diver.

An opening in the floor of this underwater lab allows divers to come and go freely.

UNDERWATER "HARD HATS"

"Dean's Patent Diving Dress" appeared in 1828. This heavy suit and helmet had windows divers could see through. Hose connections supplied air from the surface. The helmet worked as long as the diver stood upright. If the diver stooped or fell, however, the helmet quickly filled with water.

In 1840, August Siebe's "Improved Diving Dress" sealed the helmet to a full-length waterproof suit. He added an exhaust valve to the system. Siebe's apparatus became the forerunner of today's standard deep-sea diving suit.

Siebe's gear was tested. Divers wore it while

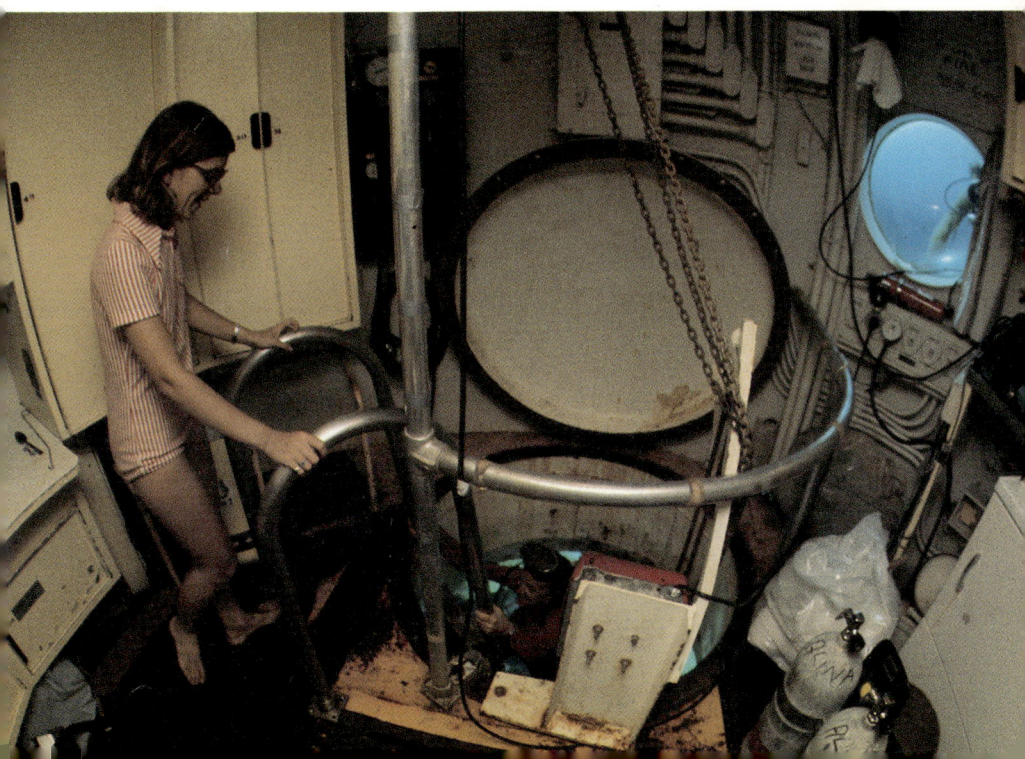

As deep sea divers travel back to the surface, they must slowly "decompress."

removing the wrecked English warship *H.M.S. Royal George*. They worked six- and seven-hour days in cold temperatures at 70-foot depths. The divers were able to breathe underwater, but every worker suffered painful problems. They had attacks of what was called "rheumatism" and "colds."

DIVING "BOXES"

At the same time, diving bells were changing. High-capacity air pumps were now being used. These pumps held enough pressure to keep water out of the bell. At first, the bell chambers were large enough to hold several men. Called "caissons," the "big boxes" became larger and larger. Soon these dimly lit, underwater dungeons were able to hold 20 or more divers. Compressed air kept them from flooding as workers dug with picks and shovels to remove mud, sand, and rock. The work was slow and dangerous, but the caisson was a leap forward for underwater construction.

But the caisson divers, like the divers who wore Siebe's gear, experienced sharp pains after returning to the surface. They were dizzy and unable to breathe well. Workers on the Brooklyn Bridge in the 1880s began calling the painful "caisson disease" the "bends."

THE BENDS

One hundred years ago people were just finding out how the bends could cripple or kill. A French doctor named Paul Bert studied the effects of pressure on the human body. He recommended that divers "decompress," or come up out of deep water, gradually. The return to the surface should be slow, he said. The slow return would let the divers' body adjust from the higher underwater pressure to normal air pressure.

This important finding led to further studies and,

finally, to decompression chambers.

In the early 1900s J.S. Haldane explained the problem. A buildup of carbon dioxide affected divers who worked in deep water for long periods. He recommended bringing divers to the surface in gradual stages to avoid pain. The greater the depth and time spent on the bottom, the more slowly a diver must ascend to the surface. Haldane's theories—with some improvements—are still used today.

DEEP DIVING NARCOSIS

In the 1920s better pumps allowed divers to work at greater depths. That improvement led to some new risks, however. At 200 feet, divers began to feel light-headed. They made mistakes and forgot why they were underwater. This was called "nitrogen narcosis."

To avoid nitrogen narcosis, a mixture of special gases is now used for deep diving. Divers are put into a pressurized chamber that has an atmosphere almost the same as the surrounding water. Once the diver is in the chamber, he is in a state of "saturation."

When saturated, a diver's body absorbs all the nitrogen it can hold. This means divers can work

The deeper the dive, the slower the diver must ascend to the surface.

underwater longer without lengthening the time they need to decompress. Saturation also helps avoid the painful bends.

17

Today, divers use SCUBA equipment, a modern version of the revolutionary Aqua-Lung.

MODERN SCUBA

Besides experiencing lightheadedness and sharp pains, there was another problem with Siebe's gear and the diving box. Both needed long hoses that connected divers on the ocean floor with an air source above the water. A system was needed that would let divers move freely and safely underwater without air from the surface.

During World War II, Jacques-Yves Cousteau and Emil Gagnon invented the "Aqua-Lung." It took divers safely to depths of 180 feet. The Aqua-Lung is familiar to us today as SCUBA (Self-Contained Underwater Breathing Apparatus).

The Aqua-Lung revolutionized diving. Anyone with proper training and equipment could now dive.

TOWS AND TENDERS

Towing devices help divers move more quickly underwater and save their strength. On a typical towing device, a diver rests his upper body against a "tow bar" or "towvane." He steers with his arms. A tow rope extends to the boat on the surface. The boat moves at a slow, steady speed. Inside the boat are the boat operator and a "tender."

The tender checks equipment and helps divers in and out of the water. He keeps lines free of the boat's propeller. The tender is responsible for the diver's safety. Many divers begin their careers as tenders.

WET SUBS

A "wet sub" is a kind of underwater convertible or pickup truck. It is a free-flooded submersible. That means it is full of water and divers breathe with SCUBA equipment. In some vehicles, four divers sit one behind the other. In others, they sit or lay

With the help of "Alvin," divers have reached depths of 13, 120 feet!

20

side by side.

Wet subs cruise large areas. They save divers time and air. Besides transporting divers, wet subs carry television cameras. Scientists from Woods Hole Oceanographic Institution survey and photograph the ocean floor. Using the U.S. Navy's Deep Submergence Vehicle "Alvin," they have dived 13,120 feet.

There in the Atlantic Ocean, they found hot water vents. The heat was intense enough to melt the plastic "socks" off Alvin. This was news! Before this, scientists only had proof of hot water vents in the Pacific.

For now, wet sub operators have to steer clear of obstructions. Charts do not always show an underwater mountain, ridge, or volcano. But technology is changing. Robert D. Ballard is a research scientist at Woods Hole who looks forward to a wet sub manned by robots instead of humans. This will expand the range of exploration.

THE BUDDY SYSTEM

It is standard procedure for divers to work in pairs or teams. Diving alone, like swimming alone, is unwise. If a diver is alone and in trouble, help is either not there or too late. The U.S. Navy considers the buddy system "the greatest single safety factor"

The buddy system means divers always work in pairs.

in its SCUBA operations. Divers working in pairs or teams can rely on themselves and on each other.

The buddy system works like this: You and your partner wear SCUBA equipment and use a tow bar. All is ready. You nod to your tender. Then you and your partner step off and go down underwater together. Once you're on the bottom, your partner leaves the tow bar. She's scouting out a kelp forest.

You stay in touch with the tow bar as you keep an eye on your buddy. Spotted goatfish and other fascinating fish swim by. You look at your console; it's almost time to leave the tow bar. You don't see your buddy so you leave the tow bar to look for her. You find her, and you both surface together.

SCUBA divers learn special hand or line-pull signals. For example, a diver whose air supply gives out will signal his partner. The partner then gives air from his own or an extra air supply. One set of signals is called ANSI (American National Standards Institute). To make the ANSI signal for danger, you stretch out your arm in the direction of the danger and clench your fist.

Suppose you are diving an area for the first time. You see an eel-like creature you can't identify. Because you don't recognize the creature, you must regard it as potentially dangerous. You signal danger to your buddy.

With the use of the buddy system and modern equipment, divers can stay underwater for longer

Hand and line-pull signals help divers communicate while underwater.

periods of time. More and more people are now making a living by working and studying underwater.

"LOCKMEN" DIVERS

George Biddle is training to be a lockman. He works for the U.S. Army Corps of Engineers. They install lock and dam systems along inland waterways like rivers. These systems must be inspected, cleaned, and repaired to operate smoothly. When lockmen dive in a river system like the Mississippi, they work in the dark. An underwater lamp can help some divers. But lockmen divers work in mud and silt. Light doesn't help them, since it merely reflects mud and silt. They have to "remember" their way.

There isn't even enough light to find tools. The lockman has to know what tools he carries in his pockets and boots. He must be skilled in using tools underwater.

Try using a hand saw underwater! You'll find it's hard to keep a straight line. You'll also learn that it's easier to pull than to push. You can't swing a hammer underwater, either. Swinging uses energy. A lockman pounds with a short sledge hammer instead. Good lockmen carry the right tool for the job.

Today's lockmen divers use tools powered by compressed air or water. When they must use electricity, they wear insulated metal helmets. These prevent shock or electrocution. They're alert to river currents, too. The currents make moving or standing hazardous.

OFF-SHORE OIL DIVERS

Massive steel and concrete structures rise out of the sea. They're oil rigs working from the ocean floor. Divers like Charlie Kluski inspect them for flaws.

Charlie knows that saltwater corrodes metal. Giant rigs and platforms are constantly battered by saltwater and waves. Even the heavy net of fishing boats can start cracks or peeling.

Working with a partner, Kluski uses high pressure hoses to blast off seaweed, barnacles, and rust from oil rig platforms.

Their work is dangerous but very important. An inspection may prevent a potential oil leak. Oil leaks and spills waste money and resources. Cleaning up oil leaks and spills costs millions of dollars. More important, companies must avoid the leaks that can harm marine life and beaches.

Some divers live on partly-submerged, three-story rigs resting on pontoons. The pontoons alone are as

Film makers need special cameras to film the fascinating underwater world.

big as submarines. Divers on the M.S.V. Stadive in the North Sea live in specially pressurized rooms on the lower deck. They stay down for four weeks without breathing ordinary air.

The divers go to work in a modern diving bell, a circular, pressurized chamber. Their work is on the seabed. Five hundred feet of black water moves above them. Here they spend 21 days in eight-hour shifts, then four more days in a decompression chamber. Then, they're flown by helicopter back to the mainland to take well earned four-week vacations.

Some off-shore oil divers are on 24-hour call and live on pipe-laying barges. Oil pipelines are being laid deeper and deeper. A repair may take the diver down to a tar-black trench. When he completes his job on the bottom, he faces cold, dull decompression stops. After his last underwater stop, he's tired and he's dragging his heavy equipment—but he isn't done. He still has to climb the 10- to 15-foot side of a rolling, windswept barge. Only then does he warm up and breathe normal air.

Off-shore oil work is hard, uncomfortable, and often dangerous. But the pay is good and, as Charlie Kluski says, "The challenge never quits."

Some salvage divers search the deep ocean depths for sunken ships— and possible treasure!

SALVAGE DIVERS

Other divers work as salvagers. Burt Webber and his team had dived wrecks to find treasure and failed. Then Webber learned about the logbook of the *Henry*, a British treasure ship that sank in 1687. Webber went to England. He studied the log and returned to the Silver Bank of the Caribbean Sea in November, 1978.

This time, his salvage crew used special devices called "cesium magnetometers" to locate the objects buried in coral. Soon the crew was finding coral-encrusted silver coins, stone olive jars, silver candlesticks, crosses, and spoons. Later, the divers recovered wooden goblets, clay pipes, ivory figures,

navigational instruments, cannons, even Chinese porcelain and gold doubloons!

In all, the salvage crew recovered treasure valued at close to $40 million. They had agreed to give half the money and many artifacts to the Dominican Republic. Other pieces went on display in museums around the world.

Not all salvage divers recover treasure like that. Mark Moncur is a salvager who works in lakes and rivers. He prefers "ice diving" to open-water diving.

He calls himself an "underwater handyman." To keep warm in frozen lakes and rivers, he wears wooly pajamas. Over them, he wears a rubberlike survival suit and SCUBA gear. He also wears thick boots and gloves with heavy liners.

Year around, this "handyman" retrieves anything, including trucks, cars, boats, motors, wallets, or handbags. Sometimes, he is called in on a rescue mission or to search for a drowning victim.

Salvage divers find treasures of many kinds!

DIVING SCIENTISTS

Diving brings scientists to the two-thirds of Earth that is underwater. For many, SCUBA diving is transportation—the only way to get to a research site.

Each dive must be planned and rehearsed in

Diving scientists study the two-thirds of the earth that is underwater.

A geologist surveys the ocean floor.

advance. Each second spent underwater counts. Time underwater costs money. It also eats up human energy.

Suppose you are standing on the deck of a small ship. The archaeological team on board hovers above the site of the oldest shipwreck known to man—a site 34 centuries old! Four years were spent just to map the site. Your expedition leader, George F. Bass, is telling about his experience with underwater time:

"I was standing upright, my diving fins resting on a rock outcrop 150 feet below the surface... The world's oldest known shipwreck lay before me, including the shapes of jars and copper ingots dating back to the 14th or early 13th century B.C. But I had no more than five minutes to plan its excavation. Five minutes to estimate the position of the ship's hull beneath its cover of sand and cargo. Five minutes to decide where to place our plexiglass dome—dubbed the 'phone booth'—in which our divers might take refuge in an emergency or telephone the surface. Five minutes to decide what mapping techniques we would use. Five minutes spent fighting nitrogen narcosis caused by breathing at such depth."

Work by George Bass and the men and women of the expedition has already changed our ideas about the Bronze Age. For example, the Bronze Age may have begun earlier than we once thought. Scientists need more years to clean and interpret the thousands of artifacts the divers recovered. These objects of bronze, gold, silver, quartz, ivory, glass, clay, copper, and bone link us to our past.

Underwater scientists find treasure in all waters. Some scientist-divers are oceanographers. They chart flow patterns and ocean basins. Some implant instruments to measure active water columns deep in the ocean. Some anchor large plastic bags at various depths in Lake Michigan, collecting water samples for different kinds of tests. One test is for the presence of mercury, which can poison fish and the people who eat them.

A marine biologist releases a tiger shark just after tagging it.

Some scientist-divers work as marine biologists. In the Galapagos Islands off the coast of Ecuador, divers study mysterious sea turtles. They discover why these huge turtles remain underwater most of their lives. Scientists have found new creatures such as blind shrimp, foot-long clams, and, in 1987, eight-

The underwater world is home to a variety of sea creatures.

foot-long, bright red worms!

Some biologists study underwater plants for new sources of food and medicine for people. Others do shark research to help us better understand shark habits and behavior.

MARINE ANIMALS THAT STING OR BITE

Lions, tigers, and bears (and cars on the highway) are more deadly than most underwater animals. Still, divers learn to be wary of certain ones. Poking fingers in pots and crevices might surprise a moray eel. The eel's powerful jaws and needle-like teeth can puncture a diver's skin.

The Portuguese man-o'-war has tentacles that often trail to 30 feet. Touching them delivers a painful sting. Even a loose, detached tentacle clinging to a diving suit after a diver leaves the water can sting.

Contrary to their reputation, sharks rarely bite humans. Very few of the many species of sharks even threaten humans, but those that do cause massive and sometimes fatal injuries.

If a diver suddenly does come upon a shark, he keeps still and avoids any sudden movement. Usually the shark will leave. If the shark stays, however, the

If a shark crosses a diver's path, he or she should avoid any sudden movement.

diver's best chance of survival is to stay on the bottom, move slowly, and hide behind a rock.

On tropical reefs, poisonous sea urchins and tropical corals give divers trouble. Sea urchins have long, brittle spines that can puncture and break off inside the diver's skin. Tropical corals can produce wounds that may not be serious, but are slow to heal. Gloves and diving suits offer some protection.

But the diver's best protection is caution—divers never provoke a sea creature!

DIVING TAKES TRAINING

It is said there are old divers and bold divers, but no old, bold divers. "Bold" means taking unnecessary risks. Many of us know someone who learned to swim by being pushed into the water. This sink-or-swim method does not carry over into diving.

Professional divers need physical and mental toughness. They need to know their equipment. They need to know how to use tools underwater. Because they know what they can and cannot do, they trust themselves. They must also trust their partners.

A number of public and private colleges, universities, and institutions offer diver training. The U.S. Navy has one of the largest programs.

The Navy trains divers in all phases of underwater operations. Navy divers are on duty in all parts of the world. They learn to repair ships, place bridge footings, do underwater construction, and perform rescue and salvage work. They train as underwater photographers and as medics.

There is considerable choice about where to take diver training. There is no choice about the *necessity* of training, however. Diving is not a do-it-yourself activity to learn from a how-to book.

SPORT DIVING

Is SCUBA diving dangerous? Yes, if you don't know what you are doing, or if you panic, or if equipment fails.

But with the proper training and reliable SCUBA or snorkel gear, diving is not dangerous. Birdwatchers above land become "fishwatchers" below water. Underwater exploring can take you to coral reefs, caves, and kelp forests. You can take pictures underwater or visit the site of a shipwreck.

Sport SCUBA diving is best in coastal areas all over the world. Some say the diver's paradise is the rainbow of corals on Australia's Great Barrier Reef, but SCUBA divers don't have to have an ocean. They can enjoy freshwater lakes, rivers, and even water-filled quarries.

Reliable equipment and training is a must, even if someone just wants to try diving once. Beginner courses in snorkeling and SCUBA diving cost about $60 to $90. Equipment costs vary, but most stores will rent SCUBA gear.

Some dealers equate the cost of SCUBA to downhill snow skiing. As in skiing, accessories, quality, location, and traveling distance all affect diving costs.

LOOKING AHEAD DOWN BELOW

Underwater vehicles can take scientists to depths impossible just 20 years ago. In 1986, Woods Hole scientists in the Navy's Alvin dove to 12,500 feet. They took some spectacular pictures. For the first time, the world saw the luxury-liner *Titanic* resting in her North Atlantic grave.

Successors to Alvin are being built. One unmanned system will have remote control. It has eyes called Argo and arms called Jason. Argo and Jason will remain deep under the ocean. This unmanned system will analyze and record what it "sees" and "touches."

Argo and Jason are loaded with instruments. They are highly complex, and their price tags are

Modern underwater research centers have helped scientists unlock the mysteries of the deep sea.

enormous. As yet, they do not replace human eyes and brains. Until they can, and at a smaller cost, unmanned vehicles will not replace human divers.

Divers will also be needed in other remote locations. Ocean "deserts"—depths at which living organisms do not exist—are being explored. These deserts are candidates for dumping biological, chemical, and nuclear waste. Not all scientists think dumping is a good idea. Ocean dumps for any waste require divers for surveying, installation, and inspection.

Other remote locations are offshore oil fields. Ocean oil drilling increases when land oil supplies decline. In a decline, more divers are needed to build and maintain rigs and platforms.

Another "location" extends around the world wherever ocean harvesting or exploration takes place. Divers gather food, medicines, and minerals from known underwater sources and look for new ones. In McMurdo Sound off Antarctica, marine biologists wear insulated "dry" suits. They drill holes and dive under the ice. They've found whole new communities—sponges, starfish, and sea spiders anchored in the ice.

More and more people are diving. How will future exploration of the underwater world proceed? Will individuals, groups, and nations use divers to compete or to cooperate? Cooperation could set a common goal: To understand, share, and protect Earth's underwater world.

FOR MORE INFORMATION

For more information on underwater diving, training, and equipment write to:

The National Association of SCUBA Diving Schools
641 West Willow Street
Long Beach, CA 90807

GLOSSARY/INDEX

ANSI 24—(American National Standards Institute) A set of hand signals that divers use to communicate underwater.

Aqua-lung 18, 19—An underwater breathing apparatus that led to modern-day SCUBA gear designed and pioneered by Jacques-Yves Cousteau and Emil Gagnon.

Bends 15—A painful, sometimes fatal, diving disorder caused by a too-rapid return from high pressure ocean depths to atmospheric pressure above the water. Also called "caisson disease" and decompression sickness.

Caisson 15—A watertight structure used in the mid 1800s for underwater construction of bridges and dams.

Compressed air 15, 26—A combination of gases free of oil contaminants and suitable for breathing while diving.

Console 24—A small instrument panel worn by a diver containing a pressure gauge, depth gauge, and compass.

Decompress 15, 17, 30—To release pressure. After a deep or long dive, divers surface slowly to release pressure put on their bodies by the water.

Diving bell 12, 14, 30—A large device for underwater work, open on the bottom and supplied with air under pressure.

GLOSSARY/INDEX

Dry suit 44—A waterproof diving suit for cold water diving. Air pumped into the suit keeps the diver dry.

Hose 13, 18, 27—A connection between a surface ship or underwater chamber and diver that provides continuous air and voice communication.

Magnetometer 31—An instrument used by divers to locate objects underwater.

Nitrogen narcosis 16, 35—A lightheaded and queasy feeling sometimes experienced by deep sea divers.

Pressure 12, 15, 27, 30—The force on a diver underwater caused by the weight of the water above and the weight of the atmosphere over the water.

Saturation 16, 17—A state in which the diver's body has absorbed all the nitrogen it can hold at a specific depth.

SCUBA 6, 19, 24, 32, 41, 42—(Self-Contained Underwater Breathing Apparatus) Open-circuit SCUBA, the most widely used system, allows divers freedom of movement underwater to limited depths. Semi-closed-circuit and closed-circuit SCUBA systems are used for deeper diving.

Sinkstone 9—A stone weighing about 40 pounds worn by pearl divers to weigh them down and

GLOSSARY/INDEX

keep them on the sea bottom.

Snorkel 41, 42 — A breathing tube that lets the diver swim on the surface, or search or survey the bottom in shallow water.

Submersible 19 — A manned or unmanned vehicle that can operate or remain underwater.

Tender 19 — A worker above the water who is responsible for diving equipment, air and tow lines, and divers' safety going in and out of the water.

Wet sub 19, 21 — A submersible vehicle filled with water used to transport divers around the ocean floor. Divers riding in a wet sub use SCUBA equipment to breathe.